Real Estate Neg

Mastering the Art of Property Deals and Maximizing Your Profits

REAL ESTATE NEGOTIATION 101

First edition. November 6, 2023.

Copyright © 2023 Andan Maharma.

ISBN: 979-8223090410

Written by Andan Maharma.

Adnan Maharma

Chapter Outline:

Introduction: The Power of Negotiation in Real Estate

- Understanding the importance of negotiation skills
- How negotiation impacts your bottom line

Setting the Stage: Researching the Market

- Conducting thorough market analysis
- Identifying target properties and their potential

Preparing for Success: Building Your Negotiation Strategy

- Defining your goals and objectives
- Assessing your leverage points

The Art of Persuasion: Effective Communication Techniques

- Active listening and empathy
- Powerful verbal and non-verbal communication

Know Your Numbers: Financial Analysis for Negotiations

- Evaluating property value and potential return on investment
- Analyzing market trends and comparable sales

Negotiating with Sellers: Finding Common Ground

- Building rapport and establishing trust
- Presenting compelling offers

Handling Multiple Offers: Strategies for Competitive Markets

- Standing out from the competition

- Tactics for winning in a bidding war

Navigating Contracts: Understanding the Legalities

- Key clauses and contingencies
- Negotiating favorable terms

Overcoming Obstacles: Dealing with Inspection and Appraisal Issues

- Addressing inspection findings
- Negotiating appraisal discrepancies

Creative Financing: Leveraging Options for Win-Win Solutions

- Exploring alternative financing methods
- Structuring creative deals

Negotiating with Tenants: Lease Agreements and Rent Renewals

- Rent negotiation tactics
- Managing tenant expectations

Collaborating with Real Estate Agents: Maximizing Their Expertise

- Building effective partnerships
- Leveraging agent negotiation skills

The Art of Influence: Negotiating with Lenders and Banks

- Securing favorable loan terms
- Negotiating loan modifications

Closing the Deal: Mastering the Final Negotiation Stage

- Negotiating closing costs and contingencies
- Sealing the agreement

Negotiating in a Challenging Market: Strategies for Economic Downturns

- Adapting to changing market conditions
- Identifying opportunities during downturns

Managing Difficult Personalities: Dealing with Tough Negotiators

- Recognizing different negotiation styles
- Techniques for handling difficult individuals

Ethical Negotiation: Balancing Profits and Fairness

- Maintaining integrity in negotiations
- Avoiding unethical practices

International Real Estate: Navigating Global Negotiations

- Understanding cultural differences
- Overcoming language and legal barriers

Negotiating for Real Estate Professionals: Enhancing Client Service

- Negotiation strategies for real estate agents and brokers
- Adding value through negotiation expertise

Lessons from Successful Real Estate Negotiators

- Case studies of renowned negotiators
- Extracting valuable lessons for your own negotiations

Chapter 1: Introduction: The Power of Negotiation in Real Estate

In the world of real estate, negotiation is a powerful tool that can make or break a deal. Whether you're a seasoned investor, a first-time homebuyer, or a real estate professional, mastering the art of negotiation is crucial for success in this competitive industry. This chapter will delve into the significance of negotiation skills and how they directly impact your bottom line.

Negotiation is more than just haggling over prices; it's an intricate dance of strategy, communication, and persuasion. By effectively negotiating, you can secure favorable terms, maximize your profits, and build strong relationships with buyers, sellers, agents, and lenders.

Understanding the importance of negotiation skills is the first step toward becoming a skilled negotiator. In real estate, every transaction involves multiple parties with differing interests and objectives. Negotiation allows you to bridge the gap between these varying perspectives and find common ground that benefits everyone involved.

Consider a scenario where you're purchasing an investment property. Without negotiation skills, you might end up overpaying or missing out on crucial concessions that could impact your return on investment. On the other hand, adept negotiation can help you secure a better purchase price, negotiate favorable financing terms, and even uncover hidden opportunities for value enhancement.

Negotiation skills impact your bottom line in a variety of ways. By understanding market dynamics, researching property values, and analyzing financial data, you can craft compelling offers that align with your investment goals. Additionally, negotiation allows you to navigate the complexities of contracts, inspections, and appraisals, ensuring that you make informed decisions and minimize risk.

Beyond financial gains, negotiation skills also enable you to build and maintain positive relationships within the real estate industry. Trust and effective communication are vital in negotiations, and by cultivating these qualities, you can establish a reputation as a fair and reliable negotiator. This, in turn, opens doors to future opportunities, referrals, and collaborative partnerships.

Throughout this book, we will explore various aspects of real estate negotiation, equipping you with the knowledge, techniques, and mindset necessary to excel in this field. Each chapter will delve into specific strategies, practical tips, and real-life examples to enhance your understanding and application of negotiation principles.

Remember, negotiation is not about winning at any cost; it's about finding mutually beneficial solutions that satisfy all parties involved. So, let's embark on this journey together and unlock the secrets of real estate negotiation, empowering you to achieve your financial goals and create lasting success in the dynamic world of real estate.

Chapter 2: Setting the Stage: Researching the Market

To embark on successful real estate negotiations, it is crucial to lay a solid foundation through thorough market analysis. In this chapter, we will explore the essential steps involved in researching the market, enabling you to identify target properties and understand their potential for optimal negotiation outcomes.

Understanding Market Dynamics

In the realm of real estate, market dynamics play a crucial role in shaping the opportunities and challenges that investors and negotiators face. By analyzing and understanding market dynamics, you can gain valuable insights into the overall health of the market, identify trends, and make informed decisions during negotiations. Let's delve deeper into this section.

Market dynamics refer to the factors that influence the supply and demand of real estate properties within a particular market. These factors can include economic conditions, population growth, employment rates, interest rates, government policies, and even social and cultural factors. By studying these dynamics, you can gain a better understanding of how the market operates and make predictions about its future trajectory.

One aspect of market dynamics is supply and demand. Understanding the balance between supply (the number of properties available for sale or rent) and demand (the number of buyers or tenants looking for properties) is crucial. A market with high demand and limited supply tends to be more favorable for sellers, as they have the upper hand in negotiations. Conversely, in a market with an oversupply of properties, buyers have more negotiating power. By analyzing the supply and demand dynamics, you can gauge the level of competition in the market and adjust your negotiation strategies accordingly.

Another important aspect of market dynamics is market cycles. Real estate markets typically go through cycles of expansion, contraction, and stabilization. During expansion phases, property values tend to rise, demand increases, and investors experience high returns. In contrast, during contraction phases, property values may decline, demand decreases, and investors face challenges. Understanding these cycles can help you time your negotiations strategically. For example, during a buyer's market (when supply exceeds demand), you may have more leverage to negotiate favorable terms and prices. In a seller's market (when demand exceeds supply), you may need to be more competitive and creative in your negotiation approach.

Market dynamics are also influenced by economic conditions. Factors such as GDP growth, employment rates, inflation, and interest rates impact the affordability of properties and the willingness of buyers to enter the market. For example, in a low-interest-rate environment, borrowing costs are lower, which may spur increased demand for real estate. On the other hand, high-interest rates may deter potential buyers, leading to decreased demand and potentially more favorable negotiation conditions for buyers.

Additionally, social and cultural factors can shape market dynamics. Demographic trends, lifestyle preferences, and shifts in population can impact the types of properties in demand and the areas that experience growth. For instance, the preferences of younger generations, such as millennials, may favor urban areas with access to amenities and public transportation. Analyzing these social and cultural dynamics can help you identify emerging market trends and align your negotiation strategies with the changing preferences of buyers or tenants.

To understand market dynamics effectively, it is crucial to gather data and conduct thorough research. Utilize real estate market reports, statistics, and analytics to gain insights into historical trends, current conditions, and future forecasts. These resources can provide valuable information on property prices, rental rates, absorption rates, and market trends specific to your target area. Additionally, leverage online platforms, government databases, and industry publications to access relevant data and stay updated on market developments.

By understanding market dynamics, you can tailor your negotiation strategies to the specific conditions of the market. For example, in a market experiencing high demand and limited supply, you may need to act quickly and be prepared to compete with other buyers. In a market with excess supply, you may have more room to negotiate on price or request additional concessions. By staying informed about market dynamics and adapting your strategies accordingly, you can position yourself for success in real estate negotiations.

Remember, market dynamics can vary from one location to another and can change over time. Regularly monitoring and analyzing market conditions will enable you to stay ahead of the curve and make informed decisions during negotiations.

Researching Local Market Conditions

Real estate is inherently local, and studying the market conditions of your target area is crucial. Start by delving into neighborhood demographics and amenities. Understand the type of residents the area attracts, their income levels, and their preferences. Additionally, analyze the proximity and quality of schools, parks, shopping centers, and transportation options. Assess the economic climate and job growth in the region, as these factors can significantly influence the demand for properties. Furthermore, investigate local development plans and infrastructure projects to identify areas of growth and potential investment hotspots.

Utilizing Real Estate Data and Tools

In today's digital age, a wealth of real estate data and tools are at your fingertips. Explore online platforms and databases specific to your market, such as real estate listing websites and market research portals. Leverage real estate market reports, statistics, and analytics to gain a comprehensive understanding of market trends. Look for data on property prices, rental rates, historical sales, and market forecasts. By incorporating data-driven insights into your analysis, you can make more accurate projections and informed decisions during negotiations.

Defining Investment Criteria

To narrow your focus and streamline your research, it is essential to define your investment criteria. Clarify your investment goals, whether it's long-term appreciation, rental income, or a combination of both.

Determine your risk tolerance and the level of involvement you seek in managing the property. Based on these considerations, determine the types of properties and investment strategies that align with your objectives. Establish key criteria such as location preferences, property size, price range, and any specific features or amenities you desire. This will help you identify properties that match your investment criteria and save time during the research process.

Identifying Target Properties

With your investment criteria in place, it's time to embark on the exciting task of identifying potential target properties. Begin by conducting property searches using various channels, including online listings, Multiple Listing Services (MLS), and real estate platforms. Utilize filters and advanced search techniques to narrow down your options based on your criteria. Consider factors such as location, property type, size, price range, and any specific features or amenities you desire. Carefully review property descriptions, photographs, and virtual tours to evaluate their suitability.

Analyzing Property Potential

Once you have identified potential properties, it's important to assess their potential value and profitability. Evaluate property appreciation potential by examining comparable sales and market trends in the area. Look at recent sales prices of similar properties and analyze the average rate of appreciation over time. Consider factors such as rental income, cash flow projections, and occupancy rates if you plan to generate rental income from the property. Additionally, assess the property's condition, potential renovation or improvement opportunities, and any value-add strategies that could enhance its market value. Furthermore, estimate expenses such as property taxes, maintenance costs, and insurance to gain a comprehensive view of the property's potential returns.

Conducting Due Diligence

Before proceeding further, it is crucial to conduct due diligence on the properties that meet your criteria. Verify property ownership and title status to ensure a clear and legal transaction. Engage the services of a professional title company or real estate attorney to conduct a thorough title search and ensure there are no encumbrances or liens on the property. Review zoning regulations and any potential restrictions that may affect property use or future development plans. Additionally, investigate any legal or environmental issues that could impact the property's value or future development potential. Thorough due diligence will safeguard your interests and minimize potential risks associated with the property.

Engaging with Local Experts

While conducting your research, it can be immensely beneficial to engage with local real estate experts. Consult with experienced real estate agents or brokers who possess in-depth knowledge of the market you are targeting. They can provide valuable insights into market trends, property valuations, and negotiation strategies. Their expertise and connections can help you navigate the intricacies of the local market and provide you with an edge during negotiations. Additionally, consider seeking guidance from other professionals such as real estate appraisers, contractors, or property managers who can provide specific expertise in their respective fields.

By following these steps and investing time in comprehensive market research, you will gain a solid understanding of the real estate landscape. Armed with this knowledge, you will be well-equipped to identify potential opportunities, assess their viability, and approach negotiations with confidence and strategic acumen. The next chapter will focus on preparing for success by building your negotiation strategy based on your research findings.

Chapter 3: Preparing for Success: Building Your Negotiation Strategy

To achieve success in real estate negotiations, it is essential to lay a strong groundwork by building a solid negotiation strategy. This chapter will guide you through the process of preparing for success by defining your goals and objectives, as well as assessing your leverage points. These critical steps will help you approach negotiations with clarity, confidence, and a strategic advantage.

Defining Your Goals and Objectives

The first step in building your negotiation strategy is to define your goals and objectives. What do you aim to achieve through the negotiation process? Are you seeking to secure the best possible price, favorable contract terms, or additional concessions? Clarifying your goals will provide you with a clear direction and help you prioritize your efforts during negotiations.

Consider your long-term investment objectives, financial targets, and risk tolerance. Are you looking for short-term gains or long-term appreciation? Do you prioritize cash flow or property value appreciation? Understanding your goals will shape your negotiation approach and guide your decision-making throughout the process.

Additionally, consider any non-financial objectives or personal preferences that may impact your negotiation strategy. Are there specific terms or conditions that are important to you, such as a quick closing timeline, flexible financing options, or specific property features? Clearly identifying your objectives will allow you to communicate with them effectively and negotiate for them during the process.

Assessing Your Leverage Points

To negotiate effectively, it is crucial to assess your leverage points—factors or strengths that give you an advantage in the negotiation process. By understanding your leverage points, you can capitalize on them to influence the outcome in your favor.

Start by identifying your strengths and assets that can strengthen your negotiating position. These may include factors such as:

Financial strength: If you have a strong financial position or access to favorable financing options, it can enhance your negotiation leverage.

Knowledge and expertise: Your knowledge of the local market, property values, and negotiation strategies can give you an edge.

Market conditions: Understanding current market dynamics, such as supply and demand, can provide valuable leverage in negotiations.

Alternatives and options: Assess any alternative properties or investment opportunities you have in mind. Having attractive alternatives can strengthen your negotiation position.

Timing: Consider timing factors that may work in your favor, such as a motivated seller, a property that has been on the market for a long time, or a desirable location that experiences limited availability.

By recognizing your leverage points, you can leverage them effectively during negotiations. Highlight your strengths, communicate them confidently, and use them as a basis for justifying your negotiation requests.

Furthermore, it is essential to identify the counterparty's potential leverage points or motivations. Assess their goals, objectives, and any potential pressures they may be facing. By understanding their position, you can tailor your negotiation strategy to address their needs and concerns effectively.

Remember that negotiation is a dynamic process, and leverage points can shift throughout the negotiation. Continuously assess the situation, adapt your strategy accordingly, and be prepared to leverage new information or changing circumstances to your advantage.

By defining your goals and objectives and assessing your leverage points, you lay the foundation for a strong negotiation strategy. This preparation allows you to enter negotiations with clarity, focus, and confidence. In the next chapters, we will delve into specific negotiation techniques, communication strategies, and tools that will further enhance your negotiation skills.

Chapter 4: The Art of Persuasion: Effective Communication Techniques

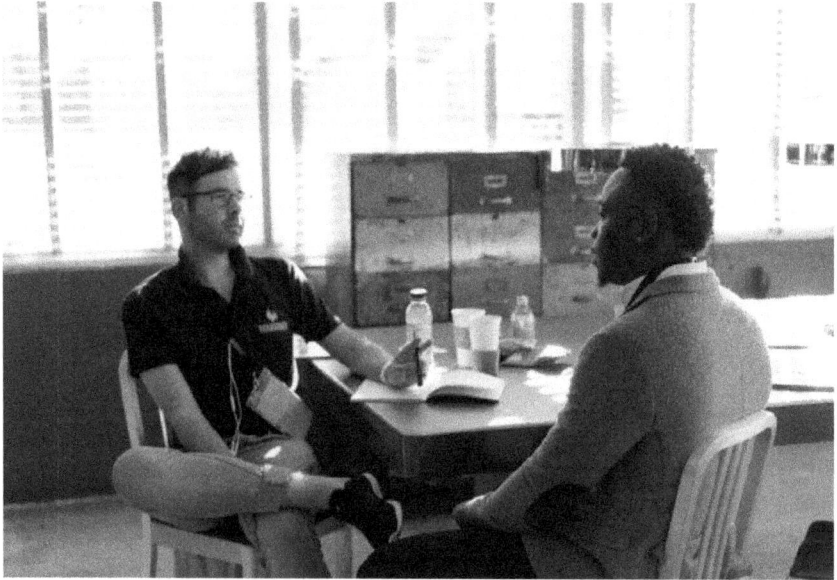

In the world of real estate negotiations, effective communication is the key to persuasion and successful outcomes. This chapter will delve into the art of persuasion, focusing on two vital communication techniques: active listening and empathy, as well as powerful verbal and non-verbal communication. By honing these skills, you will enhance your ability to understand others, convey your message effectively, and build strong rapport with the parties involved.

Active Listening and Empathy

Active listening is a fundamental skill that lays the groundwork for effective communication. It involves not only hearing the words being spoken but also fully engaging and understanding the speaker's message, tone, and body language. Practice the following techniques to become a proficient active listener:

a) Paying full attention: Give your undivided attention to the speaker, maintaining eye contact and avoiding distractions. Show genuine interest in what they are saying.

b) Paraphrasing and clarifying: Repeat or rephrase key points to demonstrate your understanding and ensure that you have captured the speaker's intended meaning. Seek clarification when needed to avoid misunderstandings.

c) Asking open-ended questions: Encourage the speaker to elaborate and provide more information by asking open-ended questions that promote dialogue and deeper understanding.

Empathy is closely tied to active listening and involves the ability to understand and share the feelings and perspectives of others. By practicing empathy, you demonstrate your genuine interest and concern, which can foster trust and rapport during negotiations. Put yourself in the other party's shoes, listen for underlying emotions, and validate their feelings. This helps create a positive negotiation environment, where both parties feel heard and understood.

Powerful Verbal Communication

Verbal communication skills play a crucial role in negotiations. Your choice of words, tone of voice, and delivery can significantly impact the outcome. Here are some techniques to enhance your verbal communication:

a) Clear and concise expression: Clearly articulate your thoughts and ideas, using simple and straightforward language. Avoid jargon or complex terms that may confuse or intimidate others.

b) Structuring your message: Organize your ideas in a logical manner, providing a clear flow of information. Use an opening statement to capture attention, present your points, and conclude with a strong closing to reinforce your message.

c) Active and assertive communication: Express your thoughts and opinions assertively, using "I" statements to take ownership of your perspective. This demonstrates confidence while maintaining respect for the other party's views.

d) Managing emotions: Stay calm and composed, even in the face of challenging or heated discussions. Emotional intelligence is crucial for maintaining a productive negotiation atmosphere.

Non-Verbal Communication

Non-verbal communication encompasses body language, facial expressions, gestures, and other non-verbal cues that convey messages without words. Pay attention to the following aspects of non-verbal communication during negotiations:

a) Eye contact: Maintain appropriate eye contact to establish rapport and show attentiveness. Avoid excessive or uncomfortable eye contact that may convey aggression or discomfort.

b) Facial expressions: Be aware of your facial expressions, ensuring they align with the message you are conveying. Smile genuinely when appropriate and display empathy through facial cues.

c) Posture and gestures: Maintain an open and confident posture, avoiding defensive or closed-off positions. Use appropriate hand gestures to emphasize key points, but avoid excessive or distracting movements.

d) Voice tone and pace: Vary your voice tone and pace to convey interest and engagement. A calm and steady tone can help maintain a positive negotiation atmosphere.

e) Mirroring and matching: Subtly mirror the body language and mannerisms of the other party, as it can help build rapport and create a sense of connection. However, be authentic and avoid overdoing it.

By mastering active listening, empathy, powerful verbal communication, and non-verbal cues, you can effectively convey your message, build rapport, and influence the negotiation process. These communication techniques foster understanding, collaboration, and trust, creating a strong foundation for successful real estate negotiations.

Chapter 5: Know Your Numbers: Financial Analysis for Negotiations

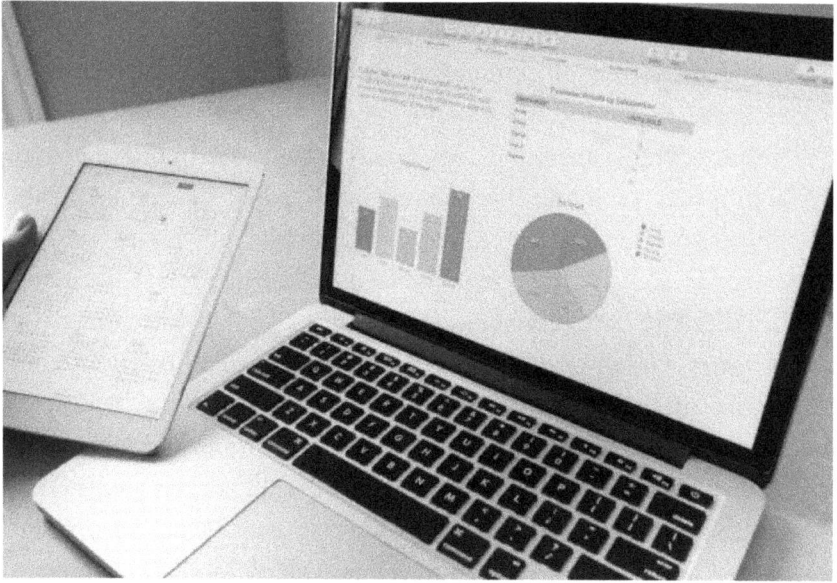

In the world of real estate negotiations, knowing your numbers is essential for making informed decisions and negotiating effectively. This chapter will focus on the importance of financial analysis and understanding key numbers to evaluate property value, potential return on investment, and market trends. By harnessing the power of data, you will be equipped with valuable insights to drive successful negotiations.

Evaluating Property Value and Potential Return on Investment

One of the primary objectives in real estate negotiations is to determine the value of a property accurately. By evaluating property value, you can gauge whether the asking price is fair and identify potential opportunities for negotiation. Consider the following factors:

a) Comparable Sales Analysis: Compare recent sales of similar properties in the area to assess the market value. Look for properties with similar characteristics such as location, size, condition, and amenities. Analyze their sale prices to derive a reasonable estimate of the property's value.

b) Income Approach: For income-generating properties, such as rental properties or commercial spaces, utilize the income approach. Evaluate the property's potential rental income, taking into account vacancy rates, operating expenses, and market rental rates. Apply appropriate capitalization rates or income multipliers to estimate the property's value based on its income-generating potential.

c) Cost Approach: In some cases, the cost approach can provide insights into property value. Assess the cost of constructing a similar property, taking into consideration land value, construction costs, and depreciation factors. While the cost approach may not be the primary method for valuing properties, it can offer additional perspective.

d) Market Factors: Consider the overall market conditions and economic factors that can influence property value. Factors such as supply and demand dynamics, interest rates, local development, and market sentiment can impact property values. Stay updated on market trends to evaluate how these factors affect property pricing.

Understanding the potential return on investment (ROI) is another critical aspect of financial analysis. By analyzing the potential ROI, you can assess the profitability of an investment and negotiate accordingly. Calculate metrics such as cash-on-cash return, cap rate, or internal rate of return (IRR) to determine the expected returns on your investment.

Analyzing Market Trends and Comparable Sales

To negotiate effectively, it is crucial to stay informed about market trends and comparable sales. Analyzing market trends provides insights into the direction of the real estate market, while comparable sales helps in assessing the competitive landscape. Consider the following steps:

a) Market Research: Continuously monitor market trends, both locally and regionally, to identify patterns and anticipate shifts. Stay updated on factors such as price fluctuations, market absorption rates, and average days on market. Analyze supply and demand dynamics to understand the market conditions and adjust your negotiation strategies accordingly.

b) Comparable Sales Analysis: Conduct a thorough analysis of recently sold properties that are comparable to the property you are negotiating on. Look for properties in the same neighborhood or similar locations with similar features and sizes. Analyze their sales prices, time on the market, and any unique factors that influenced the transactions. This analysis provides valuable insights into the recent market activity and can be used as a benchmark for negotiations.

c) Real Estate Market Reports: Leverage real estate market reports and data from reliable sources to gain comprehensive insights into market trends and comparable sales. These reports provide statistical data, charts, and analysis on property values, sales volume, and market trends. They offer a macro-level view of the real estate market and can inform your negotiation strategies.

By conducting thorough financial analysis and staying informed about market trends and comparable sales, you gain a competitive edge in negotiations. Armed with accurate property valuations, an understanding of potential returns on investment, and insights into the market, you can negotiate from an informed position. This knowledge allows you to make data-driven decisions and present compelling arguments during negotiations.

Chapter 6: Negotiating with Sellers: Finding Common Ground

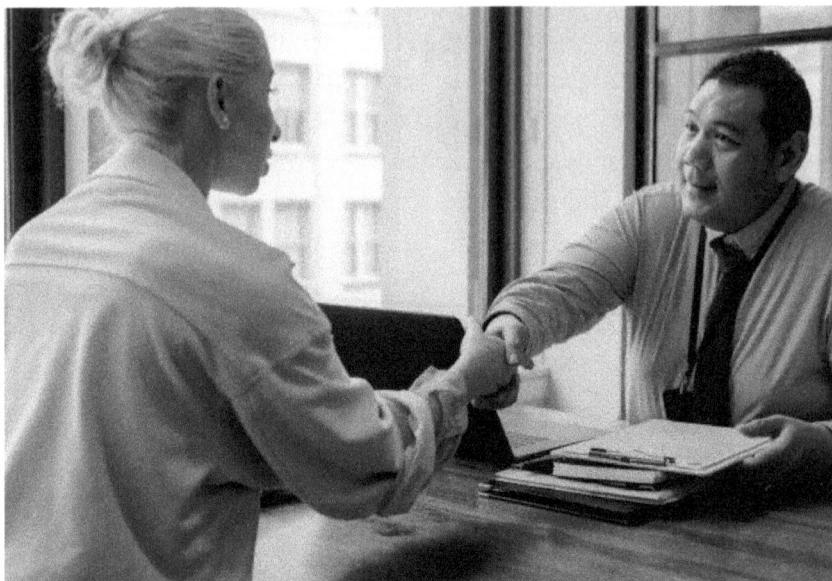

Negotiating with sellers in real estate requires the ability to build rapport, establish trust, and present compelling offers. This chapter explores strategies for finding common ground and achieving mutually beneficial outcomes during negotiations. By focusing on relationship-building and crafting irresistible offers, you can navigate the negotiation process with confidence and increase your chances of success.

Building Rapport and Establishing Trust

Building rapport with the seller is a crucial foundation for successful negotiations. Establishing a positive relationship can help create an atmosphere of trust and open communication. Consider the following strategies:

a) Active Listening: Engage in active listening by paying close attention to the seller's needs, concerns, and motivations. Show genuine interest and empathy to build a connection.

b) Empathy and Understanding: Put yourself in the seller's shoes and demonstrate empathy for their circumstances. Understand their emotional attachment to the property and any personal reasons for selling.

c) Effective Communication: Clearly communicate your intentions, objectives, and expectations to the seller. Be transparent, honest, and open in your communication, fostering trust and goodwill.

d) Highlighting Common Ground: Find common ground with the seller, such as shared values or objectives. Highlighting these shared interests can create a sense of alignment and facilitate cooperation during negotiations.

e) Professionalism and Respect: Maintain professionalism throughout the negotiation process. Treat the seller with respect and courtesy, even in the face of challenging discussions.

Presenting Compelling Offers

Crafting compelling offers is essential to gaining the seller's attention and generating interest. Your offer should stand out from competing offers and align with the seller's motivations. Consider the following techniques:

a) Research and Preparation: Thoroughly research the property, market conditions, and the seller's situation. Use this information to tailor your offer to their specific needs and circumstances.

b) Competitive Pricing: Offer a fair and competitive price based on your financial analysis and market research. Provide justification for your offer and demonstrate your understanding of the property's value.

c) Financing Pre-Approval: Obtain a pre-approval letter from a reputable lender to demonstrate your financial readiness and increase the seller's confidence in your ability to close the deal.

d) Flexible Terms: Consider including flexible terms in your offer to accommodate the seller's preferences. This may involve adjusting the closing timeline, offering a leaseback option, or accommodating specific requests that are important to the seller.

e) Personalized Touch: Add a personal touch to your offer by including a well-crafted cover letter or a brief introduction about yourself and your motivations for purchasing the property. This can help create an emotional connection and make your offer more memorable.

f) Earnest Money Deposit: Consider offering a significant earnest money deposit to demonstrate your seriousness and commitment to the transaction. A larger deposit can instill confidence in the seller and make your offer more appealing.

g) Contingencies and Due Diligence: Be mindful of the contingencies and due diligence timelines you include in your offer. Strive to strike a balance between protecting your interests and reassuring the seller that the transaction will progress smoothly.

h) Timely and Complete Documentation: Ensure that all required documentation is submitted promptly and accurately. A well-organized and complete offer package reflects your professionalism and dedication to a smooth transaction.

Remember, negotiations with sellers are often emotionally charged, as selling a property can be a significant life event. By building rapport, establishing trust, and presenting compelling offers, you can foster a cooperative atmosphere and increase the likelihood of reaching mutually beneficial agreements. The next chapter will focus on negotiating with buyers, providing strategies to navigate their perspectives and preferences effectively.

Chapter 7: Handling Multiple Offers: Strategies for Competitive Markets

In competitive real estate markets, handling multiple offers requires strategic approaches to stand out from the competition and increase your chances of success. This chapter explores effective strategies for navigating multiple offers and winning bidding wars. By employing these tactics, you can position yourself as a strong contender and secure the desired property even in a highly competitive market.

Standing Out from the Competition

In a multiple-offer scenario, it is crucial to differentiate yourself from other buyers. Consider the following strategies to make your offer more attractive:

a) Offer a Strong Purchase Price: Determine the maximum amount you are willing to pay for the property and make a competitive offer.

Conduct a thorough market analysis and consider the property's value, recent comparable sales, and market conditions to guide your pricing strategy.

b) Demonstrate Financial Strength: Provide evidence of your financial readiness to the seller. Include a pre-approval letter from a reputable lender to show that you have secured financing. If possible, offer a larger down payment or demonstrate your ability to pay in cash, which can give you a competitive edge.

c) Minimize Contingencies: Keep your offer as clean as possible by minimizing contingencies. Sellers often favor offers with fewer hurdles and faster closing timelines. However, ensure that you protect your interests and conduct appropriate due diligence within the given timeframes.

d) Flexible Closing Timeline: Tailor your closing timeline to the seller's needs whenever feasible. If the seller desires a quick closing, be prepared to accommodate their timeline. Alternatively, if the seller needs more time to find a new property or make other arrangements, consider offering a longer closing timeline or a leaseback option.

e) Personalize Your Offer: Add a personal touch to your offer by including a cover letter or a brief introduction that highlights your genuine interest in the property. Share your story, explain why the property is important to you, and express your commitment to being a responsible owner.

f) Escalation Clause: Consider including an escalation clause in your offer, which automatically increases your purchase price if competing offers are received. This can help you stay ahead of the competition without revealing your maximum offer upfront.

Tactics for Winning in a Bidding War

In intense bidding wars, it's essential to employ effective tactics to increase your chances of success. Consider the following strategies:

a) Set a Maximum Budget: Determine your absolute maximum budget for the property and stick to it. Avoid getting caught up in the excitement and emotions of the bidding war, as it can lead to overpaying or stretching beyond your financial means.

b) Act Quickly: Be prompt in submitting your offer and respond swiftly to any counteroffers or requests for additional information. Delays can give other buyers an opportunity to strengthen their offers or secure the property.

c) Increase Earnest Money Deposit: Consider offering a larger earnest money deposit to demonstrate your seriousness and commitment to the transaction. This shows the seller that you are willing to invest a significant amount upfront and have a vested interest in the property.

d) Stay in Communication: Maintain open lines of communication with the seller's agent to stay informed about the status of the bidding war. This can provide insights into the seller's preferences and help you adjust your offer accordingly.

e) Be Flexible with Terms: Remain flexible and willing to negotiate on terms that are important to the seller. This may include closing costs, inspection timelines, or other contingencies. Find ways to accommodate the seller's needs while still protecting your interests.

f) Consider an Appraisal Gap: In a competitive market, property prices may exceed appraised values. If you are confident in the property's worth and your financial ability to cover the gap between the appraised value and the purchase price, consider waiving the appraisal contingency or agreeing to cover any appraisal shortfall.

g) Leverage Your Agent's Expertise: Collaborate closely with your real estate agent, leveraging their market knowledge and negotiation skills. They can guide you through the process, provide insights into the competition, and help you make strategic decisions.

Remember, the goal is not just to win the bidding war but also to secure the property at a price that aligns with its value and your financial capacity. Stay disciplined, assess each opportunity objectively, and make informed decisions that align with your long-term goals.

By implementing these strategies for handling multiple offers and winning bidding wars, you can increase your chances of success in competitive real estate markets. The next chapter will focus on negotiating with agents, providing insights into navigating their perspectives and leveraging their expertise to your advantage.

Chapter 8: Navigating Contracts: Understanding the Legalities

Navigating contracts is a crucial aspect of real estate negotiations, as it involves understanding the legalities and ensuring that your interests are protected. This chapter will delve into key clauses and contingencies commonly found in real estate contracts and provide guidance on negotiating favorable terms. By acquiring a solid understanding of the contractual process, you can safeguard your interests and navigate negotiations with confidence.

Key Clauses in Real Estate Contracts

Real estate contracts contain several essential clauses that outline the rights, obligations, and conditions of the parties involved. Familiarize yourself with the following key clauses:

a) Purchase Price and Payment Terms: Clearly define the purchase price and the payment terms, including the amount of earnest money deposit, down payment, and financing arrangements. Specify the timeline for payment and any conditions related to the release of funds.

b) Property Description: Accurately describe the property being purchased, including its address, legal description, and any specific details that should be included in the contract.

c) Contingencies: Contingencies are provisions that allow the parties to withdraw from the contract under specific conditions. Common contingencies include financing contingency, home inspection contingency, appraisal contingency, and title contingency. Understand the implications and timelines associated with each contingency and ensure they align with your needs and protection.

d) Closing Date and Timeline: Specify the closing date and outline the timeline leading up to the closing, including the deadlines for completing due diligence, obtaining financing, and fulfilling other obligations.

e) Title and Ownership: Address matters related to title insurance, ownership rights, and any existing encumbrances or liens on the property. Ensure that the contract provides for a clear transfer of title and includes provisions for resolving any title issues.

f) Property Condition: Consider including clauses that address the condition of the property, such as a representation of its current state and any agreed-upon repairs or maintenance to be completed prior to closing.

g) Default and Remedies: Define the consequences of default by either party and outline the remedies available to the non-defaulting party, such as the right to terminate the contract or seek legal recourse.

Negotiating Favorable Terms

Negotiating favorable terms in a real estate contract can provide added protection and align the agreement with your objectives. Consider the following strategies:

a) Identify Your Priorities: Prioritize the terms that are most important to you and focus your negotiation efforts on those aspects. This may include price adjustments, specific contingencies, or desired timelines.

b) Consult with Professionals: Seek guidance from your real estate agent, attorney, or other professionals with expertise in real estate contracts. They can provide valuable insights, review the contract, and advise you on potential negotiation points.

c) Prepare a Counteroffer: If there are aspects of the contract that do not align with your preferences, prepare a counteroffer that outlines the proposed changes. Clearly articulate the reasons for the requested modifications and provide alternative language or terms that better suit your needs.

d) Leverage Market Conditions: In a buyer's market, you may have more negotiating power to request favorable terms. Conversely, in a seller's market, you may need to be more flexible in your negotiations. Stay attuned to the current market conditions to adjust your negotiation approach accordingly.

e) Be Mindful of Deadlines: Adhere to the specified timelines for counteroffers and acceptance of offers. Failing to respond within the given timeframe may result in the loss of negotiation leverage or the opportunity to negotiate further.

f) Maintain Professionalism: Approach negotiations with professionalism, courtesy, and respect for the other party. Maintaining a cooperative and collaborative mindset can foster a more productive negotiation process.

Remember that negotiation is a give-and-take process. Be prepared to compromise on certain terms while safeguarding your key interests. Collaborate closely with your real estate agent and legal professionals to ensure that the contract reflects your objectives and provides adequate protection.

By understanding the legalities involved in real estate contracts and employing effective negotiation strategies, you can navigate the contractual process with confidence and secure an agreement that safeguards your interests.

Chapter 9: Overcoming Obstacles: Dealing with Inspection and Appraisal Issues

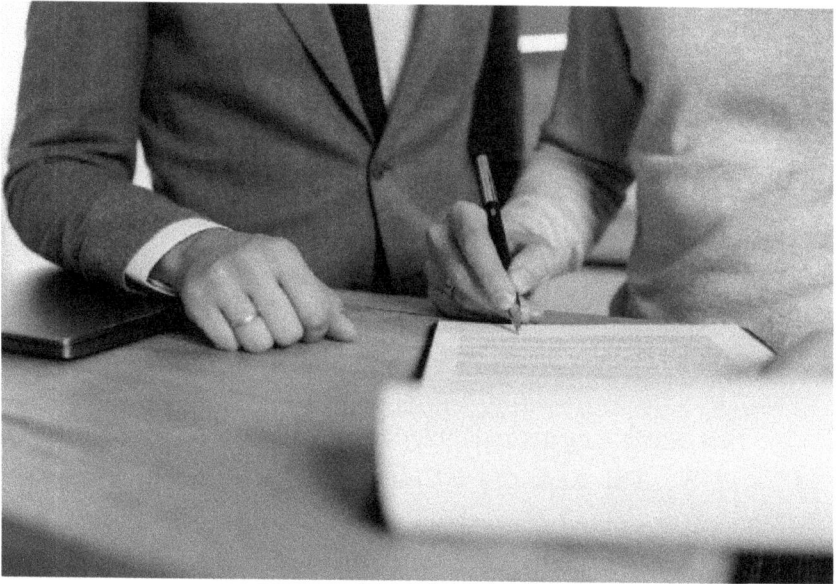

During the real estate transaction process, obstacles related to inspections and appraisals can arise. This chapter will focus on strategies for addressing inspection findings and negotiating appraisal discrepancies. By approaching these challenges proactively and effectively, you can navigate potential hurdles and ensure a successful transaction.

Addressing Inspection Findings

Inspections play a crucial role in uncovering any underlying issues with the property. When faced with inspection findings, consider the following strategies:

a) Review the Inspection Report: Carefully review the inspection report, paying close attention to significant issues and potential safety concerns. Prioritize the findings based on their severity and impact on the property's value and habitability.

b) Seek Professional Advice: Consult with professionals, such as contractors or specialists, to assess the scope and cost of addressing the identified issues. Their expertise can help you understand the necessary repairs or improvements and their associated costs.

c) Prioritize Repair Requests: Based on the inspection findings and professional advice, determine which repairs are essential and those that may be negotiable. Prioritize repair requests that are crucial for the property's safety, structural integrity, or compliance with building codes.

d) Request Repairs or Concessions: Communicate your repair requests or desired concessions to the seller through your real estate agent. Clearly outline the identified issues and explain your expectations regarding repairs or financial adjustments. Be open to negotiations and consider potential compromises to reach a mutually agreeable solution.

e) Negotiate a Seller Concession: If the seller is unwilling or unable to make the requested repairs, negotiate for a concession or credit towards closing costs or the purchase price. This can help offset the cost of addressing the identified issues after the transaction closes.

Negotiating Appraisal Discrepancies

Appraisal discrepancies occur when the appraised value of the property differs from the agreed-upon purchase price. To address these discrepancies, consider the following strategies:

a) Review the Appraisal Report: Carefully review the appraisal report and understand the factors that influenced the appraiser's valuation. Look for potential errors or inaccuracies that may have affected the appraised value.

b) Assess Comparative Market Analysis (CMA): Conduct a comparative market analysis using recent sales data and market trends to support your position regarding the property's value. Present this information to the seller or the seller's agent to support your case for a higher value.

c) Consider a Second Opinion: In certain circumstances, you may request a second appraisal if you believe the initial appraisal was inaccurate or incomplete. Consult with your real estate agent and lender to understand the process and feasibility of obtaining a second opinion.

d) Renegotiate the Purchase Price: If the appraisal comes in lower than the purchase price, renegotiate with the seller to adjust the price to reflect the appraised value. Communicate the appraisal findings and provide supporting evidence to support your request for a price reduction.

e) Seek Additional Financing Options: If the renegotiation of the purchase price is unsuccessful, explore alternative financing options, such as increasing your down payment or seeking additional financing from a different lender. This may bridge the gap between the appraised value and the purchase price.

f) Reconsider Your Options: If negotiations regarding appraisal discrepancies are unfruitful, evaluate whether the property's value aligns with your financial objectives. You may need to consider alternatives, such as renegotiating the terms, walking away from the transaction, or exploring other available properties.

Navigating inspection and appraisal issues requires effective communication, negotiation skills, and a willingness to find mutually agreeable solutions. Collaborate closely with your real estate agent, consult with professionals, and approach these challenges with a problem-solving mindset. By addressing these obstacles head-on, you can work towards a successful transaction and protect your interests.

Chapter 10: Creative Financing: Leveraging Options for Win-Win Solutions

In real estate negotiations, creative financing options and deal structures can often lead to win-win solutions for both parties involved. This chapter explores alternative financing methods and strategies for structuring creative deals. By leveraging these options, you can overcome financing obstacles, expand your opportunities, and reach mutually beneficial agreements.

Exploring Alternative Financing Methods

Traditional financing methods may not always meet the unique needs of every real estate transaction. By exploring alternative financing methods, you can expand your options and find solutions that align with the specific circumstances of the deal. Consider the following approaches:

a) Seller Financing: Seller financing involves the seller acting as the lender, providing a loan to the buyer to facilitate the purchase. This option can be beneficial when traditional financing is challenging to obtain or when both parties see value in the arrangement. Negotiate the loan terms, including interest rate, repayment schedule, and any security or collateral required.

b) Lease-to-Own: A lease-to-own agreement allows a tenant to lease the property with the option to purchase it at a later date. This arrangement provides flexibility for the buyer to test the property before committing to ownership, while the seller benefits from consistent rental income and a potential sale in the future. Clarify the terms of the lease, purchase price, option period, and how the rent payments will be applied towards the purchase.

c) Assumable Mortgages: An assumable mortgage allows the buyer to take over the existing mortgage of the seller, subject to the lender's approval. This option can be advantageous if the seller has a favorable interest rate or terms that are advantageous compared to current market conditions. Ensure that you understand the terms of the assumed mortgage, any fees involved, and seek the necessary approval from the lender.

d) Hard Money Lenders: Hard money lenders provide short-term loans typically based on the value of the property rather than the borrower's creditworthiness. This option can be useful when quick financing is needed or when traditional lenders are not available. Understand the terms, interest rates, and repayment schedule associated with hard money loans, as they generally come with higher interest rates and shorter repayment periods.

Structuring Creative Deals

In addition to alternative financing, structuring creative deals can unlock opportunities and address specific needs or challenges. Consider the following strategies:

a) Joint Ventures: Joint ventures involve partnering with another party, such as an investor or developer, to pool resources, share risks, and collaborate on a real estate project. Each party brings complementary skills, expertise, or financial contributions to the venture. Clearly define the roles, responsibilities, profit sharing, and exit strategies within a joint venture agreement.

b) Equity Sharing: Equity sharing arrangements allow multiple parties to share ownership in a property. This can be beneficial when one party lacks the necessary funds for a full purchase. Determine the percentage of ownership and establish the terms of profit sharing, responsibilities for expenses, and exit strategies.

c) Seller Concessions: Negotiate with the seller for concessions that can benefit both parties. This may include credits towards closing costs, repairs, or other financial incentives that can improve the terms of the deal without affecting the purchase price.

d) Land Contracts: A land contract, also known as a contract for deed or installment sale agreement, involves the buyer making installment payments to the seller while occupying and using the property. This option can be suitable for buyers who may not qualify for traditional financing or when the seller prefers a steady stream of income. Clearly outline the terms, payment schedule, interest rate, and conditions for transferring title upon completion of payments.

e) Exchange Programs: Explore the possibility of participating in 1031 exchanges or other tax-deferred exchange programs. These programs allow you to sell a property and reinvest the proceeds into another property, deferring capital gains taxes. Engage with qualified intermediaries and follow the rules and regulations governing these exchanges.

When considering alternative financing methods and structuring creative deals, it is essential to consult with professionals, including real estate agents, attorneys, and financial advisors. They can provide guidance, ensure compliance with legal requirements, and help you evaluate the risks and benefits associated with these options.

By leveraging alternative financing methods and structuring creative deals, you can overcome financing challenges, expand your investment opportunities, and create win-win solutions for all parties involved.

Chapter 11: Negotiating with Tenants: Lease Agreements and Rent Renewals

Lease agreements and rent renewals are critical aspects of maintaining a harmonious relationship with tenants. This chapter focuses on cultivating positive tenant relationships by employing effective negotiation strategies for lease agreements and rent renewals. By fostering open communication, understanding tenant perspectives, and finding mutually beneficial solutions, you can ensure smooth negotiations and tenant satisfaction.

Rent Negotiation Strategies

Rent negotiations require a delicate balance of assertiveness and empathy. Employ the following strategies when negotiating rent with tenants:

a) Market Research: Conduct thorough market research to determine the current rental rates in your area. Understanding the local market allows you to set reasonable rental expectations and engage in informed discussions with tenants about rental prices.

b) Tenant Evaluation: Assess the value that tenants bring to your property. Consider factors such as their payment history, length of tenancy, and overall responsibility as tenants. Recognize and appreciate tenants who consistently fulfill their lease obligations and maintain the property well.

c) Lease Review: Familiarize yourself with the terms of the lease agreement. Identify any provisions that allow for rent adjustments or lease renewals. This knowledge provides a solid foundation for discussions and ensures compliance with legal requirements.

d) Open Communication: Maintain open lines of communication with tenants throughout the negotiation process. Encourage them to share their concerns or needs regarding the rental price. Listen attentively and demonstrate empathy to understand their perspective.

e) Offer Value-Added Services: Consider providing additional services or amenities to justify a rent increase. This could include upgraded appliances, improved maintenance services, or access to shared facilities. Present these enhancements as added value to the tenant's living experience.

f) Flexible Lease Terms: Explore alternatives to a rent increase, such as offering a longer lease term or providing flexibility in the payment schedule. This flexibility can appeal to tenants who value stability or need adjustments to accommodate their financial situation.

Managing Tenant Expectations

Effectively managing tenant expectations is crucial for maintaining positive relationships and successful negotiations. Consider the following strategies:

a) Proactive Communication: Regularly communicate with tenants about lease renewal timelines, policies, and expectations. Provide them with ample notice regarding rent adjustments or lease renewal options. This proactive approach promotes transparency and minimizes surprises.

b) Transparency in Rent Adjustments: Clearly explain the factors that influence rent adjustments, such as increased operating costs or market conditions. Sharing this information helps tenants understand the rationale behind the proposed changes and fosters trust.

c) Tenant Feedback: Encourage tenants to provide feedback on their rental experience. Actively listen to their suggestions and concerns, and address them promptly and professionally. By incorporating tenant input, you demonstrate a commitment to their satisfaction and well-being.

d) Fair and Consistent Treatment: Treat all tenants fairly and consistently. Avoid making exceptions or granting special privileges to one tenant over others, as this can create animosity and dissatisfaction among tenants. Apply lease terms and policies consistently to foster a sense of fairness.

e) Professionalism in Negotiations: Approach negotiations with professionalism and respect. Remain calm and composed, even in challenging discussions. Strive to find common ground and work towards a solution that benefits both parties.

By employing these strategies, you can cultivate positive tenant relationships and navigate lease agreements and rent renewals with ease. Remember, fostering open communication and understanding tenant perspectives are key to successful negotiations and tenant satisfaction.

Chapter 12: Collaborating with Real Estate Agents: Maximizing Their Expertise

Collaborating with real estate agents is instrumental in navigating the complexities of the real estate market. This chapter explores strategies for building effective partnerships with agents and leveraging their negotiation skills to maximize outcomes. By capitalizing on their expertise, you can enhance your negotiating position and achieve successful results.

Building Effective Partnerships

Establishing a strong partnership with a real estate agent is essential for a successful real estate transaction. Consider the following strategies to build effective partnerships:

a) Clear Communication: Establish open lines of communication from the outset. Clearly communicate your goals, expectations, and preferences to your agent. Likewise, provide feedback and updates to ensure both parties are aligned throughout the process.

b) Trust and Transparency: Foster trust and transparency with your agent. Share relevant information about your financial situation, desired property features, and any specific concerns or preferences. This enables your agent to better understand your needs and tailor their approach accordingly.

c) Regular Updates: Maintain regular communication with your agent, ensuring you receive updates on market conditions, new listings, and any relevant changes that may impact your real estate goals. Regular updates help you stay informed and enable your agent to provide tailored recommendations.

d) Collaborative Decision-Making: Involve your agent in the decision-making process. Leverage their market knowledge and expertise to weigh different options, assess risks, and make informed decisions. By working collaboratively, you can tap into their insights and benefit from their experience.

e) Respect Professional Boundaries: Recognize and respect the professional boundaries of your agent. They are there to guide and assist you, but it is important to understand that they may have limitations based on ethical and legal considerations. Be mindful of their expertise and trust their guidance.

Leveraging Agent Negotiation Skills

Real estate agents possess invaluable negotiation skills that can greatly enhance your position in negotiations. Consider the following ways to leverage their expertise:

a) Pricing Strategy: Rely on your agent's market knowledge and pricing expertise to determine the appropriate offer price or listing price for a property. They can conduct comparative market analysis, evaluate market trends, and advise you on the optimal pricing strategy.

b) Counteroffer Management: When faced with counteroffers, leverage your agent's negotiation skills to navigate the back-and-forth discussions effectively. They can advocate on your behalf, respond to counteroffers, and negotiate terms that align with your objectives.

c) Emotional Detachment: Agents can bring a level of emotional detachment to negotiations, which is vital for maintaining a rational and objective approach. They can help you navigate emotions, avoid impulsive decisions, and focus on achieving the best possible outcome.

d) Creative Solutions: Agents often have a repertoire of creative solutions for complex negotiation scenarios. They can propose alternative terms, contingencies, or concessions that may help bridge gaps and facilitate agreements between parties.

e) Transaction Management: Agents excel at managing the intricacies of the transaction process. They can handle paperwork, coordinate inspections, liaise with lenders, and ensure that all necessary documentation is in order. This allows you to focus on the negotiation aspects while trusting your agent to handle the logistics.

f) Mediation and Conflict Resolution: In cases where conflicts arise during negotiations, agents can act as mediators to find common ground and facilitate resolution. Their communication skills and ability to navigate challenging conversations can help diffuse tensions and maintain productive negotiations.

By collaborating effectively with real estate agents and leveraging their negotiation skills, you can capitalize on their expertise and maximize your outcomes. Building a strong partnership with your agent and utilizing their market knowledge and negotiation acumen positions you for success in the real estate arena.

Chapter 13: The Art of Influence: Negotiating with Lenders and Banks

Negotiating with lenders and banks requires finesse and strategic approaches to secure favorable loan terms and navigate loan modifications. This chapter delves into the art of influence when dealing with lenders and provides strategies for negotiating favorable loan terms and seeking loan modifications. By mastering these skills, you can strengthen your position and achieve the best possible outcomes in your financial transactions.

Securing Favorable Loan Terms

When seeking a loan from lenders or banks, employ the following strategies to secure favorable loan terms:

a) Research and Prepare: Thoroughly research various lenders and loan options to understand the current market rates, terms, and conditions. This knowledge empowers you to negotiate from an informed position. Prepare a strong application with accurate financial information, compelling business plans (if applicable), and any other supporting documents requested by the lender.

b) Enhance Your Creditworthiness: Strengthen your creditworthiness by ensuring a good credit score, addressing any negative credit issues, and improving your overall financial profile. A strong credit history and financial stability increase your negotiating power and improve the chances of obtaining favorable loan terms.

c) Highlight Your Financial Strengths: Emphasize your financial strengths, such as a stable income, valuable assets, or a significant down payment. Demonstrating your ability to repay the loan and mitigating the lender's perceived risks can help negotiate more favorable terms.

d) Leverage Multiple Offers: If possible, approach multiple lenders simultaneously to obtain competing loan offers. This allows you to compare terms and negotiate with lenders who may be more inclined to offer favorable conditions to secure your business.

e) Negotiate Interest Rates and Fees: Engage in discussions with lenders about interest rates, origination fees, closing costs, and other associated fees. Request rate reductions or fee waivers based on market conditions, your creditworthiness, or the strength of your financial position.

f) Seek Professional Guidance: Consult with a qualified mortgage broker or financial advisor who can provide guidance on the negotiation process. These professionals have expertise in navigating lender negotiations and can offer insights and strategies tailored to your specific situation.

Negotiating Loan Modifications

When facing financial challenges and seeking loan modifications, employ the following strategies to negotiate effectively:

a) Open Communication: Initiate early and open communication with your lender when facing financial difficulties. Clearly explain your situation, providing relevant documentation to support your claims.

Maintaining transparency builds trust and increases the likelihood of reaching a mutually beneficial agreement.

b) Understand Loan Modification Options: Familiarize yourself with available loan modification programs, such as interest rate reductions, term extensions, principal forbearance, or loan refinancing. Assess which options align with your needs and financial goals.

c) Present a Strong Case: Prepare a compelling case for loan modification, highlighting the reasons behind your financial challenges and the steps you have taken to address them. Demonstrate your commitment to fulfilling your obligations and your ability to make modified payments.

d) Provide Supporting Documentation: Submit comprehensive financial documentation, including bank statements, tax returns, income statements, and any other relevant records that validate your financial circumstances. This documentation strengthens your case and enhances your credibility.

e) Seek Professional Assistance: Engage the services of a reputable loan modification attorney or housing counselor experienced in negotiating with lenders. These professionals can provide guidance, negotiate on your behalf, and ensure compliance with legal requirements.

f) Persistence and Follow-Up: Be persistent and follow up regularly with your lender to stay updated on the status of your loan modification request. Document all communications and maintain a record of important dates, discussions, and agreements reached during the negotiation process.

Remember that negotiating with lenders and banks requires patience, resilience, and a collaborative approach. By mastering the art of influence, conducting thorough research, and seeking professional guidance, you can increase your chances of securing favorable loan terms and successfully negotiating loan modifications that align with your financial needs.

Chapter 14: Closing the Deal: Mastering the Final Negotiation Stage

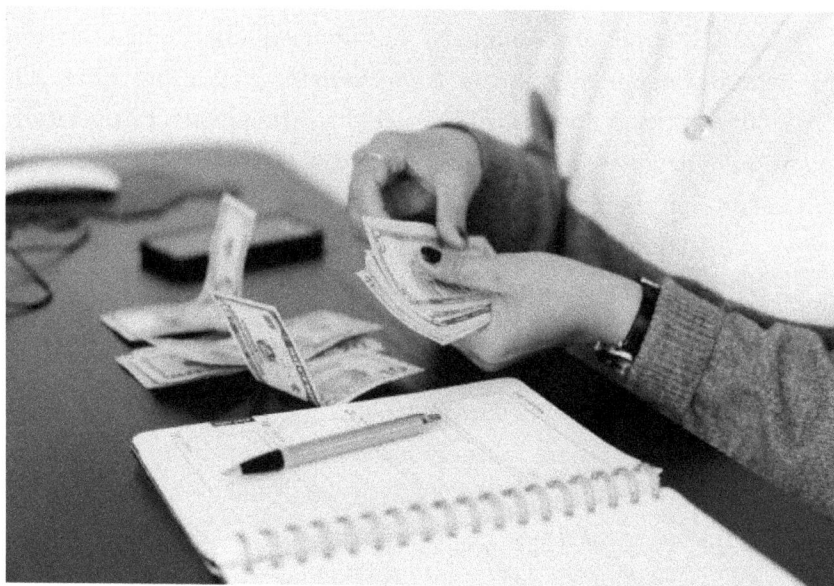

The final negotiation stage of a real estate transaction plays a crucial role in ensuring a successful closing. This chapter focuses on mastering the art of negotiation when it comes to closing costs, contingencies, and sealing the agreement. By skillfully navigating these aspects, you can finalize the deal with confidence and achieve your desired outcomes.

Negotiating Closing Costs

Closing costs are expenses incurred during the transfer of property ownership. When negotiating closing costs, consider the following strategies:

a) Research and Compare: Research typical closing costs in your area and compare estimates from different service providers, such as lenders, title companies, and inspectors. Armed with this information, you can negotiate for more competitive rates or request cost breakdowns to ensure transparency.

b) Request Seller Concessions: Negotiate with the seller to cover a portion of the closing costs. This can be done by requesting a seller concession in the purchase agreement or proposing a higher purchase price that accounts for the anticipated closing costs.

c) Shop for Service Providers: Exercise your right to select service providers for various closing-related tasks, such as title insurance, inspections, and appraisals. Obtaining multiple quotes and comparing fees can provide leverage for negotiation.

d) Seek Lender Assistance: Consult with your lender to explore options for reducing or rolling closing costs into the loan amount. Some lenders may offer incentives or closing cost credits that can help mitigate your out-of-pocket expenses.

e) Clarify Responsibility: Ensure that the division of closing costs between the buyer and seller is clearly defined in the purchase agreement. Negotiate and clarify which party will be responsible for specific costs, such as property taxes, title insurance, or attorney fees.

Addressing Contingencies

Contingencies are conditions or events that must be met for the transaction to proceed. Skillfully addressing contingencies can help alleviate concerns and provide assurance to both parties. Consider the following strategies:

a) Thoroughly Understand Contingencies: Familiarize yourself with the contingencies outlined in the purchase agreement, such as financing, inspection, or appraisal contingencies. Understand the deadlines and conditions associated with each contingency.

b) Prompt Completion of Contingencies: Act diligently to meet the requirements of the contingencies within the specified timelines. Timely completion demonstrates your commitment to the transaction and enhances your negotiating position.

c) Negotiate Contingency Removal: If you have successfully fulfilled a contingency, such as obtaining financing or completing inspections, consider negotiating the removal of that specific contingency. This can help strengthen your position and signal to the seller that you are committed to proceeding with the transaction.

d) Request Repairs or Concessions: If inspection contingencies uncover significant issues, negotiate with the seller for repairs or concessions that address the concerns. Clearly document the agreed-upon resolutions and ensure they are included as addendums to the purchase agreement.

e) Communicate Contingency Fulfillment: Promptly communicate with the seller or their agent when contingencies are met. Provide the necessary documentation or evidence to satisfy the requirements and demonstrate your readiness to proceed to the closing stage.

Sealing the Agreement

Sealing the agreement involves finalizing the terms, signing the necessary documents, and ensuring a smooth transition to the closing process. Consider the following strategies:

a) Review Final Documents: Thoroughly review all final documents, including the purchase agreement, addendums, and any amendments or disclosures. Seek clarification on any ambiguous or confusing terms before signing.

b) Engage Legal Assistance: If necessary, consult with a real estate attorney to review the closing documents and provide guidance. They can help identify any potential legal issues and ensure that your interests are protected throughout the process.

c) Communicate Clearly: Maintain open and clear communication with all parties involved, including the seller, their agent, your agent, and any service providers. Respond promptly to requests for information or documentation to avoid delays in the closing process.

d) Conduct a Final Walkthrough: Schedule a final walkthrough of the property to ensure that it is in the agreed-upon condition and that any repairs or negotiated changes have been satisfactorily addressed.

e) Prepare for Closing: Gather all necessary documentation and funds required for the closing. Work closely with your lender, attorney, or escrow agent to ensure a smooth and timely closing process.

f) Celebrate Success: Once the closing is complete, congratulate yourself and celebrate the successful conclusion of the negotiation process. Take pride in achieving your real estate goals and moving forward with your plans.

By skillfully negotiating closing costs, effectively addressing contingencies, and ensuring a seamless agreement sealing process, you can finalize the deal with confidence and satisfaction. Keep lines of communication open, maintain a solution-oriented mindset, and work collaboratively with all parties involved to achieve a successful closing.

Chapter 15: Negotiating in a Challenging Market: Strategies for Economic Downturns

Navigating a challenging market during economic downturns requires a unique set of strategies and adaptability. This chapter focuses on effective negotiation tactics for such situations, including adapting to changing market conditions and identifying opportunities amidst downturns. By mastering these strategies, you can position yourself for success and achieve favorable outcomes even in the face of economic challenges.

Adapting to Changing Market Conditions

In challenging market conditions, it is essential to adapt your negotiation approach to align with the changing dynamics. Consider the following strategies:

a) Research and Market Analysis: Conduct thorough research and stay updated on the current market conditions. Understand trends, pricing fluctuations, and changes in buyer or seller behavior. This knowledge equips you to make informed decisions and tailor your negotiation strategies accordingly.

b) Pricing and Market Positioning: Assess the market value of properties and adjust your pricing and market positioning accordingly. This may involve pricing properties more competitively to attract buyers or positioning yourself as an attractive buyer by offering competitive terms and conditions.

c) Flexibility in Negotiation Terms: Be flexible in negotiating terms such as closing dates, contingencies, or repairs. This flexibility can help you stand out in a competitive market and accommodate the needs and concerns of the other party.

d) Open Communication: Maintain open lines of communication with the other party involved in the negotiation. Foster transparency and honesty to build trust and facilitate mutually beneficial discussions. Clear communication helps manage expectations and resolve potential conflicts more effectively.

e) Creative Solutions: Explore creative solutions that can benefit all parties involved. This may include considering alternative financing options, lease-to-own agreements, or other innovative approaches that align with the current market conditions.

Identifying Opportunities during Downturns

While economic downturns present challenges, they also create opportunities for those who can identify them. Consider the following strategies to uncover opportunities:

a) Market Research: Conduct extensive market research to identify areas or sectors that may be more resilient during economic downturns. Look for potential growth sectors, emerging markets, or undervalued properties that may present favorable investment opportunities.

b) Distressed Sales and Foreclosures: Keep an eye out for distressed sales and foreclosed properties that may be available at discounted prices. Be prepared to act quickly and engage in negotiations with motivated sellers or financial institutions.

c) Off-Market Deals: Network with industry professionals, including real estate agents, investors, and developers, to learn about off-market deals. These deals are not listed publicly and may provide unique opportunities to negotiate favorable terms.

d) Seller Motivation: Identify sellers who may be motivated to negotiate due to financial pressures or other circumstances. Distressed sellers, retirees, or those facing a change in personal circumstances may be more open to negotiation and flexible on terms.

e) Value-Add Properties: Seek properties with potential for value appreciation through renovations, repositioning, or development. These properties may be undervalued in the current market but have the potential to yield significant returns in the future.

f) Government Incentives and Programs: Stay informed about government incentives or programs designed to stimulate the real estate market during economic downturns. These initiatives may provide financial assistance, tax benefits, or favorable financing terms that can enhance your negotiation position.

g) Partnerships and Joint Ventures: Explore opportunities for partnerships or joint ventures with investors or developers who have the resources and expertise to capitalize on market opportunities. Collaborating with experienced professionals can help mitigate risks and maximize returns.

By adapting to changing market conditions and actively seeking opportunities during economic downturns, you can position yourself for success. Embrace flexibility, remain proactive in your research, and maintain a solution-oriented mindset. Through effective negotiation strategies and a keen eye for emerging opportunities, you can navigate challenging markets and achieve favorable outcomes.

Chapter 16: Managing Difficult Personalities: Dealing with Tough Negotiators

Negotiating with tough negotiators and managing difficult personalities can be a challenging aspect of the negotiation process. This chapter focuses on recognizing different negotiation styles and provides techniques for effectively handling difficult individuals. By understanding their tactics and employing appropriate strategies, you can maintain control, foster productive discussions, and achieve favorable outcomes.

Recognizing Different Negotiation Styles

Recognizing different negotiation styles is crucial in understanding the approach of tough negotiators. Consider the following common negotiation styles:

a) Competitive/Aggressive: Aggressive negotiators are focused on winning at all costs. They may employ intimidation tactics, high-pressure techniques, and extreme demands to gain an advantage.

b) Collaborative/Problem-Solving: Collaborative negotiators aim for win-win solutions by focusing on mutual interests, exploring creative options, and building relationships. They seek to understand the other party's perspective and find common ground.

c) Avoidant/Passive: Avoidant negotiators prefer to avoid conflicts and may be hesitant to engage in direct confrontation or assertiveness. They may avoid addressing tough issues or delay decision-making.

d) Assertive/Balanced: Assertive negotiators strike a balance between being cooperative and assertive. They advocate for their interests while maintaining respect for the other party. They actively engage in discussions and strive for mutually beneficial outcomes.

Techniques for Handling Difficult Individuals

When dealing with tough negotiators and difficult personalities, employ the following techniques to effectively manage the situation:

a) Maintain Emotional Control: Stay calm, composed, and professional during the negotiation process. Keep emotions in check, as difficult individuals may try to provoke or manipulate you. Maintaining emotional control enhances your decision-making abilities and prevents unnecessary conflicts.

b) Active Listening: Practice active listening to demonstrate that you value the other party's perspective. Seek to understand their underlying interests, concerns, and motivations. Listening attentively can help diffuse tension and open up avenues for productive discussions.

c) Empathy and Rapport Building: Cultivate empathy by putting yourself in the shoes of the other party. Seek common ground and build rapport by finding shared interests or goals. Developing a positive relationship can ease tensions and create a more collaborative atmosphere.

d) Set Boundaries: Establish clear boundaries and assert your limits when dealing with difficult individuals. Communicate your expectations and maintain firmness in enforcing them. This helps ensure that negotiations remain fair and respectful.

e) Focus on Interests, Not Positions: Shift the focus from positions to underlying interests. Encourage open dialogue about the needs and concerns of both parties. By understanding the underlying motivations, you can identify potential solutions that satisfy those interests.

f) Separate People from the Problem: Emphasize that the negotiation is about resolving the issue at hand and not a personal attack. Refrain from personalizing conflicts and maintain a problem-solving mindset. This approach helps create a more collaborative and constructive negotiation environment.

g) Use Objective Criteria: Rely on objective criteria, market data, or industry standards to support your arguments and proposals. Having verifiable facts and benchmarks helps counter difficult negotiators who rely on subjective or manipulative tactics.

h) Maintain Patience and Flexibility: Remain patient and adaptable when negotiating with tough negotiators. Be willing to explore alternative solutions or creative compromises to reach a mutually satisfactory outcome. A flexible approach can help break deadlocks and move negotiations forward.

i) Seek Mediation or Third-Party Assistance: If negotiations reach an impasse or become excessively challenging, consider involving a neutral third party, such as a mediator or arbitrator, to facilitate discussions. Their impartial perspective can help bridge gaps and resolve conflicts.

Handling difficult negotiators requires a combination of effective communication, emotional intelligence, and strategic thinking. By recognizing different negotiation styles and employing appropriate techniques, you can navigate challenging personalities and foster a productive negotiation environment.

Chapter 17: Ethical Negotiation: Balancing Profits and Fairness

Negotiation is not only about achieving favorable outcomes; it is also about conducting oneself ethically and maintaining a sense of fairness throughout the process. This chapter delves into the importance of ethical negotiation practices and provides strategies for balancing profits with fairness. By upholding integrity and avoiding unethical practices, you can build trust, preserve relationships, and achieve long-term success in negotiations.

Maintaining Integrity in Negotiations

Maintaining integrity is a cornerstone of ethical negotiation. Here are strategies for upholding integrity throughout the negotiation process:

a) Honesty and Transparency: Be honest and transparent in your communication. Avoid misrepresentation, exaggeration, or concealing information. Provide accurate and complete information to all parties involved, enabling them to make informed decisions.

b) Fulfilling Commitments: Honor your commitments and fulfill your promises. If you agree to specific terms or conditions during negotiations, ensure that you follow through on those commitments. Reliability and trustworthiness are essential for building strong relationships.

c) Respecting Confidentiality: Respect the confidentiality of sensitive information shared during negotiations. Do not disclose or misuse confidential information for personal gain or to undermine the other party. Safeguarding confidentiality fosters trust and strengthens your reputation.

d) Avoiding Deceptive Tactics: Steer clear of deceptive or manipulative tactics that can compromise fairness. Examples include false statements, hidden agendas, or exploiting the other party's vulnerabilities. Focus on constructive and transparent communication that promotes mutual understanding.

e) Professionalism and Respect: Maintain professionalism and treat all parties with respect and dignity. Avoid personal attacks, derogatory language, or aggressive behavior. Engage in constructive discussions that focus on the issues at hand.

Avoiding Unethical Practices

To promote fairness and ethical conduct in negotiations, it is crucial to avoid unethical practices. Consider the following strategies:

a) Price Fixing or Collusion: Do not engage in price-fixing or collusion with competitors to manipulate market prices or restrict competition. Uphold fair market practices and comply with antitrust laws.

b) Bribery and Corruption: Never offer or accept bribes or engage in corrupt practices. These actions undermine the integrity of negotiations and can have severe legal and ethical consequences. Adhere to anti-bribery laws and regulations.

c) Misrepresentation or False Promises: Avoid misrepresenting facts or making false promises to manipulate the other party's decision-making. Ensure that all statements and representations are accurate and truthful.

d) Unfair Advantage: Refrain from seeking unfair advantages through unethical means. This includes exploiting personal relationships, using confidential information improperly, or engaging in activities that undermine the principles of fairness.

e) Discrimination and Bias: Treat all parties equitably and avoid discrimination based on race, gender, religion, nationality, or any other protected characteristics. Base decisions and negotiations on merit, facts, and objective criteria.

f) Conflict of Interest: Disclose any potential conflicts of interest that may influence your decision-making or compromise your impartiality. Act in the best interest of all parties involved and avoid situations that may give rise to conflicts.

g) Ethical Negotiation Tactics: Utilize negotiation tactics that promote fairness and collaboration. Seek mutually beneficial solutions, practice active listening, and focus on problem-solving rather than manipulation or coercion.

By upholding integrity and avoiding unethical practices, you contribute to a positive and ethical negotiation environment. Demonstrating fairness, transparency, and professionalism enhances your credibility, builds trust with others, and fosters long-term relationships. Remember that ethical negotiation not only benefits your reputation but also contributes to the overall well-being and sustainability of the business ecosystem.

Chapter 18: International Real Estate: Navigating Global Negotiations

Engaging in international real estate negotiations requires a deep understanding of cultural differences, as well as the ability to overcome language and legal barriers. This chapter explores strategies for navigating global negotiations, ensuring effective communication, and fostering successful outcomes across diverse cultural contexts. By embracing cultural sensitivity and employing practical techniques, you can thrive in international real estate negotiations.

Understanding Cultural Differences

Cultural differences significantly influence negotiation dynamics in international real estate transactions. Here are strategies for understanding and navigating cultural differences:

a) Cultural Research: Conduct thorough research on the cultural norms, values, and business practices of the target country or region.

Understand how negotiation styles, decision-making processes, and relationship-building practices vary across cultures.

b) Cultural Sensitivity: Cultivate cultural sensitivity and demonstrate respect for cultural practices and customs. Be open-minded, adaptable, and willing to learn from the cultural perspectives of the other party. Avoid making assumptions or generalizations based on your own cultural background.

c) Relationship Building: Prioritize relationship building, as it plays a crucial role in many cultures. Invest time in establishing personal connections, engaging in social interactions, and demonstrating genuine interest in the other party's culture. Building trust and rapport paves the way for successful negotiations.

d) Communication Styles: Adapt your communication style to align with the cultural norms of the other party. Some cultures may value indirect communication, while others prefer direct and assertive approaches. Listen actively, observe non-verbal cues, and adjust your communication style accordingly.

e) Decision-Making Processes: Recognize that decision-making processes can vary across cultures. In some cultures, decisions are made collectively, while in others, they are made by individuals in positions of authority. Understand and respect the decision-making structure of the other party's culture.

Overcoming Language and Legal Barriers

In international real estate negotiations, language and legal barriers can pose challenges. Here are strategies for overcoming these barriers:

a) Language Support: Engage the services of professional translators or interpreters to ensure accurate and effective communication. Language support can help bridge the linguistic gap and prevent misunderstandings that may arise due to language barriers.

b) Legal Expertise: Seek legal expertise from professionals familiar with the legal systems and regulations of the target country or region. Local legal counsel can provide guidance on legal requirements, contract terms, and any specific considerations relevant to the international real estate transaction.

c) Written Translations: Ensure that all important documents, including contracts, agreements, and disclosures, are accurately translated into the appropriate language. Avoid relying solely on verbal communication and prioritize written translations to ensure clarity and avoid misunderstandings.

d) Cross-Cultural Communication Skills: Develop cross-cultural communication skills to navigate language and cultural differences effectively. Practice active listening, ask clarifying questions, and seek feedback to confirm mutual understanding.

e) Patience and Flexibility: Cultivate patience and flexibility when navigating language and legal barriers. Recognize that the negotiation process may require additional time and effort due to translation and legal considerations. Remain open to compromise and seek mutually acceptable solutions.

f) Cultural Liaisons: Consider engaging cultural liaisons or local experts who have a deep understanding of both the cultural nuances and legal landscape. These individuals can provide invaluable insights, bridge communication gaps, and facilitate smoother negotiations.

g) Leverage Technology: Embrace technology tools and platforms that aid in overcoming language barriers, such as real-time translation apps or video conferencing platforms with built-in language support. Utilize online resources to access legal information and templates specific to the target country or region.

By understanding cultural differences, embracing cultural sensitivity, and effectively overcoming language and legal barriers, you can navigate international real estate negotiations with confidence. Cultivate relationships, seek professional support, and remain adaptable throughout the process. By doing so, you can build successful international real estate transactions and forge valuable connections across global markets.

Chapter 19: Negotiating for Real Estate Professionals: Enhancing Client Service

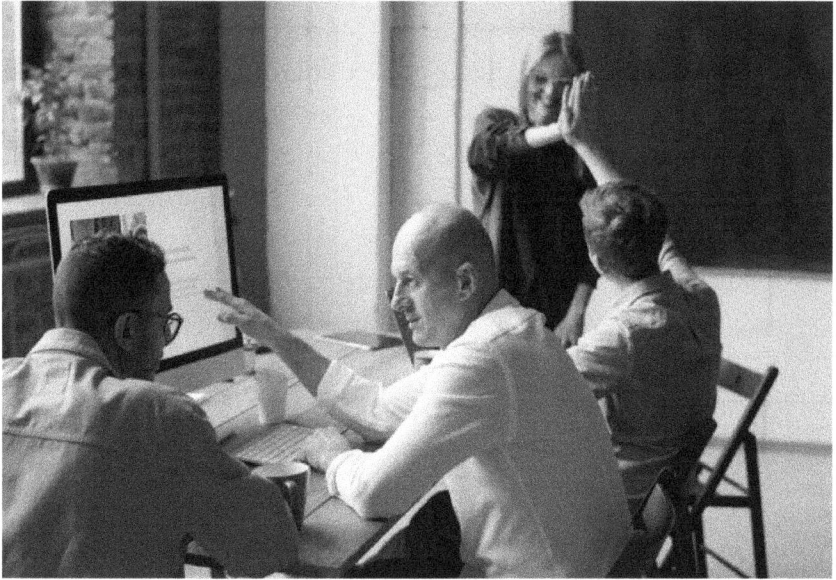

Real estate professionals play a pivotal role in the negotiation process, advocating for their clients' interests and facilitating successful transactions. This chapter explores negotiation strategies tailored specifically for real estate agents and brokers, empowering them to enhance client service and add value through their negotiation expertise. By mastering these strategies and leveraging their knowledge, real estate professionals can elevate their client service and achieve optimal outcomes.

Understanding the Negotiation Landscape

Real estate professionals must have a comprehensive understanding of the negotiation landscape to effectively represent their clients. Consider the following strategies:

a) Market Knowledge: Stay up-to-date with current market conditions, trends, and pricing dynamics. Understanding the local market empowers you to provide accurate guidance to clients and negotiate effectively on their behalf.

b) Comparable Sales Analysis: Conduct thorough comparable sales analysis to determine the fair market value of properties. This analysis helps clients make informed decisions and strengthens your negotiation position when presenting offers or counteroffers.

c) Client Needs Assessment: Conduct a detailed assessment of your clients' needs, preferences, and goals. Understanding their motivations and priorities enables you to tailor negotiation strategies that align with their best interests.

Effective Negotiation Strategies

Real estate professionals can employ various negotiation strategies to maximize client outcomes. Consider the following approaches:

a) Competitive Positioning: Assess the competition and position your clients strategically to gain an advantage in negotiations. Highlight unique selling points, such as desirable features of the property or favorable financing terms, to differentiate your clients' offers.

b) Preparation and Documentation: Thoroughly prepare all necessary documentation, including offer letters, disclosures, and contingencies, with attention to detail. Well-prepared documents demonstrate professionalism and attention to the transaction's legal and contractual aspects.

c) Active Listening and Communication: Practice active listening to understand the needs and concerns of the other party. Effective communication builds rapport and facilitates collaboration, increasing the likelihood of finding mutually beneficial solutions.

d) Creative Problem-Solving: Encourage creative problem-solving to address potential roadblocks or challenges. Brainstorm alternative solutions that can meet both parties' interests and contribute to a successful negotiation outcome.

e) Negotiating Win-Win Solutions: Strive for win-win solutions that satisfy the needs of both parties. By focusing on mutually beneficial outcomes, you foster positive relationships and build a reputation as a skilled negotiator who prioritizes fairness.

Adding Value through Negotiation Expertise

Real estate professionals can differentiate themselves by providing added value through their negotiation expertise. Consider the following strategies:

a) Education and Expertise: Continuously invest in your professional development by expanding your knowledge of negotiation techniques, industry trends, and legal regulations. Position yourself as a knowledgeable advisor who can guide clients through complex negotiations.

b) Market Insights and Analysis: Offer clients in-depth market insights, including pricing trends, inventory levels, and emerging opportunities. By providing informed analysis, you equip clients with a competitive edge in negotiations.

c) Risk Management: Mitigate potential risks by identifying and addressing them proactively. Educate clients about potential pitfalls in negotiations, such as contingencies, legal issues, or financing challenges, and guide them through strategies to mitigate those risks.

d) Network and Partnerships: Build a strong network of industry professionals, including lenders, attorneys, inspectors, and contractors. These relationships allow you to provide clients with referrals to trusted professionals, adding value to their real estate transaction experience.

e) Negotiation Representation: Offer clients skilled negotiation representation, emphasizing your ability to navigate complex negotiations on their behalf. Highlight your track record of successful outcomes and showcase testimonials from satisfied clients.

By employing effective negotiation strategies, continuously enhancing your negotiation expertise, and adding value through market insights and professional support, you can elevate your client service as a real estate professional. By doing so, you position yourself as a trusted advisor who provides guidance, maximizes client outcomes, and establishes long-lasting relationships based on exceptional negotiation expertise.

Chapter 20: Lessons from Successful Real Estate Negotiators

Learning from the experiences of successful real estate negotiators can provide invaluable insights and strategies to elevate your own negotiation skills. In this chapter, we delve into case studies of renowned negotiators in the real estate industry and extract valuable lessons that can be applied to your own negotiations. By studying their approaches, techniques, and mindset, you can enhance your negotiation practices and achieve greater success in your real estate endeavors.

Case Study 1: Jane Anderson - Mastering Effective Communication

Jane Anderson, a respected real estate negotiator, has attributed her success to mastering effective communication. She emphasizes the following lessons:

a) Active Listening: Jane practices active listening, allowing her to understand the needs, motivations, and concerns of the other party. By actively engaging and demonstrating empathy, she establishes rapport and builds trust.

b) Clarity and Conciseness: Jane understands the importance of clear and concise communication. She articulates her points effectively, ensuring that her messages are easily understood by all parties involved.

c) Non-Verbal Communication: Jane recognizes the significance of non-verbal communication, such as body language and facial expressions. She pays attention to these cues to gauge the other party's reactions and adjust her approach accordingly.

Case Study 2: John Richards - Mastering Creative Problem-Solving

John Richards, a renowned real estate negotiator, is known for his ability to find creative solutions to complex problems. Valuable lessons can be learned from his approach:

a) Out-of-the-Box Thinking: John embraces out-of-the-box thinking and encourages unconventional approaches to problem-solving. He explores alternative solutions that go beyond traditional methods, enabling him to find mutually beneficial outcomes.

b) Collaboration and Cooperation: John believes in fostering a collaborative and cooperative atmosphere during negotiations. He encourages all parties to contribute ideas and work together to find innovative solutions.

c) Flexibility and Adaptability: John remains flexible and adaptable, willing to adjust his strategies and explore new possibilities. He understands that rigid adherence to preconceived notions can limit creative problem-solving.

Case Study 3: Sarah Johnson - Mastering Emotional Intelligence

Sarah Johnson, a highly regarded real estate negotiator, emphasizes the importance of emotional intelligence in negotiations. Valuable lessons can be derived from her approach:

a) Self-Awareness: Sarah possesses a high level of self-awareness, allowing her to understand her own emotions, triggers, and biases. This self-awareness enables her to maintain emotional control during negotiations.

b) Empathy and Perspective-Taking: Sarah actively seeks to understand the other party's perspective and demonstrates empathy. By putting herself in their shoes, she can identify common ground and foster constructive discussions.

c) Conflict Resolution: Sarah excels in resolving conflicts by addressing underlying emotions and finding mutually acceptable resolutions. She prioritizes maintaining positive relationships while achieving desired outcomes.

REAL ESTATE NEGOTIATION 101

By studying the approaches of successful real estate negotiators like Jane Anderson, John Richards, and Sarah Johnson, you can extract valuable lessons for your own negotiations. Embrace effective communication, master creative problem-solving techniques, and cultivate emotional intelligence. By incorporating these lessons into your negotiation practices, you can enhance your skills, build stronger relationships, and achieve greater success in your real estate negotiations.

In conclusion, this book has provided a comprehensive exploration of the world of real estate negotiation. From understanding the power of negotiation to navigating challenging markets, managing difficult personalities, and enhancing client service, you have gained valuable insights and strategies to excel in real estate negotiations. By applying these principles and lessons, you can negotiate with confidence, integrity, and skill, ultimately achieving optimal outcomes in your real estate endeavors.

9 798223 090410